We hope this book has been informative and helpful on your journey to understanding and celebrating older adults. Thank you for your interest and support!

Title: The Birth of Meme Coins: Exploring the Pre-2017 Crypto Landscape
Subtitle: From Dogecoin to PepeCash, a journey through the early days of memetic cryptocurrencies

Series: The Rise of Meme Coins: Exploring the Pre-2017 Crypto Landscape
By Alexander C. Blair

Table of Contents

Introduction

What are meme coins?

Meme coins are a type of cryptocurrency that have gained popularity in recent years, particularly in the wake of the rise of Bitcoin and other mainstream cryptocurrencies. As the name suggests, these coins are inspired by internet memes, which are images or videos that are often humorous or satirical in nature and are widely shared across social media platforms.

Meme coins typically have low market caps and are often created as a joke or as a way to capitalize on a particular meme or trend. They are often created using a fork of an existing cryptocurrency, with changes made to the code to reflect the unique features of the meme coin.

One of the key features of meme coins is their community-driven nature. Unlike mainstream cryptocurrencies like Bitcoin and Ethereum, which are often backed by large corporations or financial institutions, meme coins are typically created and managed by small groups of enthusiasts. These communities are often very active on social media platforms like Twitter and Reddit, where they share memes, discuss the latest developments in the meme coin space, and work to promote the coin to a wider audience.

Another important aspect of meme coins is their volatility. Because these coins are often created as a joke or as a way to capitalize on a particular trend, their prices can be extremely volatile. This means that investors who are interested in meme coins need to be prepared for significant price swings, both up and down.

Despite their often humorous origins and their volatile nature, meme coins have become an increasingly important part of the cryptocurrency landscape. As more and more investors look to diversify their portfolios and take advantage of the opportunities presented by cryptocurrencies, meme coins are likely to continue to play an important role in the space. However, investors should always be careful when investing in meme coins and should do their own research to ensure that they are making informed investment decisions.

The early days of cryptocurrency and meme culture

The early days of cryptocurrency and meme culture go hand in hand. In fact, some might argue that meme culture played a crucial role in the birth of cryptocurrencies, particularly meme coins.

The early days of cryptocurrency can be traced back to the creation of Bitcoin by the anonymous person or group known as Satoshi Nakamoto in 2009. Bitcoin was created as a decentralized digital currency that allowed for peer-to-peer transactions without the need for intermediaries like banks. Bitcoin's success in the early days of crypto paved the way for other cryptocurrencies to emerge.

However, the adoption and popularity of cryptocurrencies were still limited to tech enthusiasts and early adopters in the early days. It was only in 2013 that cryptocurrencies started to gain mainstream attention, partly due to the rise of meme culture.

Meme culture refers to the internet phenomenon of creating and sharing humorous and often satirical images, videos, and texts that spread virally online. Memes have become an integral part of internet culture, and they have been used to mock and satirize everything from politics to pop culture.

In the early days of crypto, memes played a significant role in raising awareness and promoting cryptocurrencies. The most notable example of this is Dogecoin. Dogecoin started as a joke in 2013, inspired by the popular Doge meme featuring a Shiba Inu dog. The creators of Dogecoin, Billy Markus and Jackson Palmer, created the coin as a lighthearted alternative to Bitcoin.

Dogecoin's success can be attributed in large part to its association with meme culture. The Dogecoin community quickly grew, and the coin gained a cult following. Dogecoin's viral popularity helped raise awareness of cryptocurrencies, particularly among younger audiences who were not previously interested in investing in traditional finance.

Other cryptocurrencies like BBQCoin, NyanCoin, and HoboNickels also emerged in the early days of crypto, inspired by various internet memes. These meme coins gained a cult following, and although many of them did not survive in the long run, they played a crucial role in shaping the crypto landscape.

In conclusion, the early days of cryptocurrency and meme culture are intertwined, and memes played a significant role in promoting cryptocurrencies like Dogecoin to a wider audience. The rise of meme coins highlights the power of internet culture and its ability to shape new emerging markets.

Why are meme coins important to the crypto landscape?

Meme coins have become an integral part of the crypto landscape, and it is essential to understand why they are important. At first glance, meme coins may seem like a joke, but they represent a significant development in the cryptocurrency world.

Meme coins have a unique ability to capture the attention of a large audience, especially among younger generations who are active on social media. They can quickly go viral and generate a lot of interest, creating a hype that attracts investors and traders. This hype can result in significant price movements, and meme coins can experience tremendous gains in a short period.

Meme coins also have the potential to bring new users into the crypto world. They are often easier to understand than traditional cryptocurrencies, and their use cases are usually straightforward. Meme coins can also provide a gateway for those who are new to the space to learn about cryptocurrencies and how they work.

Moreover, meme coins represent a new and innovative way to approach finance. The world of cryptocurrency has always been about challenging the traditional financial system, and meme coins take this concept to the next level. They challenge the status quo of what constitutes value and what can be considered an investment. Meme coins allow anyone to participate in the financial markets, regardless of their background or financial situation.

Meme coins can also drive innovation in the crypto industry. The development of meme coins requires creative thinking and a willingness to take risks. Developers must think outside the box to create a coin that can capture the attention of the masses. This creative thinking can lead to the development of new technologies and innovative solutions that can benefit the entire crypto ecosystem.

In summary, meme coins are important to the crypto landscape because they have the potential to attract new users, drive innovation, and challenge the traditional financial system. While they may seem like a joke, they represent a significant development in the world of cryptocurrency. Investors and traders should take them seriously and understand their potential impact on the crypto market.

Chapter 1: Dogecoin, Dogecoin, launched in 2013, USD 88 billion ATH in May 2021

History and origin of Dogecoin

Dogecoin is one of the most famous meme coins to date, having gained a significant following since its creation in 2013. But how did Dogecoin come to be, and what was its original purpose?

In late 2013, two software engineers, Billy Markus and Jackson Palmer, were both interested in the emerging world of cryptocurrency. They began discussing the possibility of creating their own cryptocurrency, but they wanted it to be different from the others that were already available. They wanted something that would be fun and accessible for everyone, rather than just for those who were already deep into the world of finance and technology.

Around the same time, the internet was experiencing a surge in popularity for memes, particularly those featuring the Shiba Inu dog breed. Markus and Palmer were both fans of the doge meme, which featured a Shiba Inu dog with captions written in broken English. They decided to combine their love for cryptocurrency and memes and create a new cryptocurrency called Dogecoin.

Dogecoin was initially launched as a joke, with a logo featuring the famous doge meme and a supply of 100 billion coins. The creators made it clear from the beginning that it was not meant to be taken seriously, and they even added a disclaimer to the website warning users not to invest too much money in the currency.

Despite this, Dogecoin quickly gained a following, particularly on social media platforms like Twitter and Reddit. The community surrounding Dogecoin was fun and lighthearted, with users creating memes and jokes about the currency. In fact, the community was so active that they raised funds to sponsor the Jamaican bobsled team for the 2014 Winter Olympics, bringing Dogecoin into the mainstream media spotlight.

As Dogecoin's popularity grew, so did its value. The currency began trading on cryptocurrency exchanges, with its value fluctuating based on supply and demand. Over time, Dogecoin became more than just a joke, with many people using it for online transactions and even accepting it as payment for goods and services.

Today, Dogecoin remains one of the most popular meme coins on the market, with a market capitalization of over $50 billion at its peak in May 2021. While its original creators may not have intended for it to become a serious investment vehicle, its success shows the power of community and the importance of having a lighthearted approach to technology and finance.

The role of the Dogecoin community in its success

Dogecoin's success can be attributed to its community, which has played a significant role in its growth and development. The Dogecoin community is unique in that it is highly supportive and inclusive, with a strong focus on promoting charitable causes and spreading positivity.

The community was born out of the Dogecoin subreddit, which was created shortly after the coin's launch in 2013. The subreddit quickly grew in popularity, and it became a hub for Dogecoin enthusiasts to share news, tips, and memes related to the coin.

One of the defining features of the Dogecoin community is its emphasis on humor and lightheartedness. The coin's creators intentionally designed it to be a playful and fun alternative to the more serious and technical cryptocurrencies that dominated the market at the time.

As a result, the community has embraced this spirit and has created a wide range of memes, jokes, and parodies related to Dogecoin. Some of the most popular memes include the "Doge" image, which features a Shiba Inu dog with broken English captions, and the "Dogeza" pose, which involves kneeling and bowing in a gesture of respect and submission.

Beyond its humor, the Dogecoin community has also gained a reputation for its charitable efforts. In 2014, the community raised over $30,000 worth of Dogecoin to help send the Jamaican bobsled team to the Sochi Winter Olympics. Since then, the community has continued to support a variety of charitable causes, including funding clean water wells in developing countries and supporting children's hospitals.

The community's generosity and altruism have helped to create a positive image of Dogecoin and have attracted a loyal following of users and investors. This has, in turn, helped to drive up the coin's value and increase its mainstream acceptance.

Overall, the Dogecoin community has been a key factor in the coin's success, helping to promote it, build its reputation, and drive its adoption. Its unique culture and values have helped to set it apart from other cryptocurrencies and have made it a beloved and enduring part of the crypto landscape.

Dogecoin's technical features and limitations

Dogecoin, like other cryptocurrencies, is a decentralized digital currency that operates on a peer-to-peer network. It is based on the popular "Doge" meme and was created as a "joke" by programmers Billy Markus and Jackson Palmer in December 2013. Despite its origins, Dogecoin quickly gained popularity, thanks in part to its unique technical features.

One of the key features of Dogecoin is its mining algorithm, which uses Scrypt technology. This algorithm is designed to prevent ASIC miners from dominating the network and allow regular users to mine Dogecoin with their computers or laptops. This feature made Dogecoin more accessible to the general public, unlike other cryptocurrencies such as Bitcoin that require specialized hardware to mine.

Another important feature of Dogecoin is its fast transaction times. Transactions are processed quickly due to the block time of one minute, which is much faster than Bitcoin's ten-minute block time. Additionally, Dogecoin has a block reward of 10,000 coins per block, which is much higher than Bitcoin's 6.25 coins per block.

Despite its unique features, Dogecoin also has some limitations. One of the main limitations is its lack of development activity. Dogecoin's development team is small and consists mainly of volunteers, which means that new features and updates are slow to be released. This can make Dogecoin less attractive to businesses and individuals who require more advanced features.

Another limitation of Dogecoin is its lack of a fixed supply. Unlike Bitcoin, which has a fixed supply of 21 million coins, Dogecoin has an unlimited supply. This means that new Dogecoins are continuously being created, which could potentially lead to inflation and a decrease in the coin's value over time.

In addition, Dogecoin has been criticized for its lack of real-world use cases. While some businesses accept Dogecoin as payment, its adoption rate is still relatively low compared to other cryptocurrencies. This could be due in part to its origins as a meme and the perception that it is a "joke" cryptocurrency.

Overall, Dogecoin's technical features have played a significant role in its success. Its accessibility, fast transaction times, and high block rewards have made it popular among cryptocurrency enthusiasts. However, its lack of development activity and fixed supply could pose challenges in the long term.

Dogecoin's use cases and real-world adoption

Dogecoin is a cryptocurrency that started as a joke but has become a cultural phenomenon. Despite its humorous origins, Dogecoin has a number of real-world use cases and has been adopted by several businesses and organizations.

One of the most significant use cases of Dogecoin is as a means of transaction. The low fees associated with Dogecoin make it an attractive option for merchants and buyers alike. In fact, Dogecoin was used as a form of payment for the Jamaican bobsled team in the 2014 Winter Olympics.

Dogecoin has also been used for charitable causes. The Dogecoin community has a reputation for being generous and has raised funds for a number of different causes, including disaster relief efforts and clean water initiatives. In 2014, the Dogecoin community raised over $30,000 to send the Jamaican bobsled team to the Winter Olympics.

In addition to charitable causes, Dogecoin has been used for tipping content creators and internet personalities. This use case is particularly popular on social media platforms such as Twitter and Reddit, where users can tip each other for creating and sharing content.

Another use case for Dogecoin is as a store of value. While Dogecoin was created as a joke, its growing popularity has led some people to invest in it as a long-term investment. The low fees and fast transaction times associated with Dogecoin make it an attractive option for those looking to store their wealth in a digital currency.

Overall, Dogecoin's use cases and real-world adoption have played a significant role in its success. Its low fees, fast transaction times, and charitable nature have made it a popular option for transactions, tipping, and investment. As the cryptocurrency landscape continues to evolve, it will be interesting to see how Dogecoin and other meme coins are utilized in the future.

The rise of Dogecoin in the crypto market

The rise of Dogecoin in the crypto market has been nothing short of spectacular. Despite starting off as a joke, the cryptocurrency has managed to capture the imagination of millions of people around the world and has become a household name in the world of digital currencies. This section will explore the factors that contributed to the rise of Dogecoin in the crypto market.

1. The Power of Social Media Dogecoin's meteoric rise in popularity can be largely attributed to its presence on social media platforms. In particular, the Dogecoin community on Reddit and Twitter played a significant role in promoting the cryptocurrency and creating a sense of community around it. Memes featuring the Shiba Inu dog, which is the face of Dogecoin, went viral on these platforms, helping to raise awareness of the cryptocurrency.

2. Celebrity Endorsements Dogecoin received a massive boost in popularity when several high-profile celebrities endorsed the cryptocurrency on social media. Elon Musk, the CEO of Tesla and SpaceX, has been one of the most vocal supporters of Dogecoin, tweeting about it frequently and even referring to himself as the "Dogefather". Other celebrities, including Snoop Dogg and Mark Cuban,

have also expressed their support for the cryptocurrency, helping to boost its profile and attract new investors.

3. Accessibility and Affordability Another key factor in Dogecoin's rise to prominence is its accessibility and affordability. Unlike Bitcoin, which can be quite expensive to purchase, Dogecoin is relatively cheap, with a current value of just a few cents per coin. This makes it an attractive option for new investors who are looking to get started with cryptocurrency but don't want to invest large amounts of money.

4. Support from Online Retailers Dogecoin's growing popularity has also been helped by the fact that several online retailers now accept the cryptocurrency as a form of payment. This includes websites such as eGifter and AllGamer, which allow users to purchase gift cards using Dogecoin. The fact that more retailers are accepting the cryptocurrency as a legitimate form of payment has helped to boost its credibility and increase its overall value.

5. The Power of the Meme Finally, it's important to acknowledge the power of the meme in driving the popularity of Dogecoin. The cryptocurrency was created as a joke, and its success can be largely attributed to the fact that it has become a cultural phenomenon. The use of memes has helped to create a sense of community around Dogecoin,

with many investors feeling a sense of camaraderie and belonging to the community.

In conclusion, the rise of Dogecoin in the crypto market can be attributed to a combination of factors, including the power of social media, celebrity endorsements, accessibility and affordability, support from online retailers, and the use of memes. While some may view Dogecoin as a fad or a passing trend, there's no denying that it has made a significant impact on the world of cryptocurrency and has captured the imagination of millions of people around the world.

Chapter 2: Rare Pepe Party, Counterparty, launched in 2016, USD 2.8 million ATH in Mar 2017

The history and origin of Rare Pepe Party

The Rare Pepe Party (RPP) is a meme-based cryptocurrency that was launched in 2016 on the Counterparty platform. It was one of the earliest examples of meme coins and gained significant attention from the crypto community due to its unique use case and connection to the Pepe meme.

The Pepe meme has a long history on the internet and became a cultural phenomenon in the early 2010s. It was created by artist Matt Furie as part of his comic series, "Boy's Club," and depicts a green frog with a smug expression. The meme gained popularity on forums like 4chan and Reddit and became a symbol of internet culture and humor.

In 2016, a group of developers created the Rare Pepe Wallet, a digital wallet that allowed users to store and trade rare Pepe cards as assets on the blockchain. The Rare Pepe Wallet was built on top of the Counterparty platform, a decentralized exchange that uses the Bitcoin blockchain.

The Rare Pepe Wallet was designed to be a platform for buying, selling, and trading rare Pepe cards as assets. Each Pepe card was unique and had its own value, determined by the rarity and popularity of the meme on which it was based. Users could buy and sell Pepe cards using RPP, the native cryptocurrency of the platform.

The Rare Pepe Wallet quickly gained a following among collectors and traders of rare Pepe cards. The platform hosted regular auctions and sales of rare Pepe cards, and prices for some of the most sought-after cards reached thousands of dollars.

Despite its popularity, the Rare Pepe Wallet faced some challenges during its development. The use of the Pepe meme in the platform's branding and marketing attracted criticism from some members of the meme community who felt that the project was exploiting the meme for financial gain. Additionally, the project faced regulatory hurdles due to the uncertain legal status of cryptocurrencies and the potential for RPP to be considered a security.

Despite these challenges, the Rare Pepe Party continued to grow and gain recognition in the crypto community. The platform's success paved the way for other meme-based cryptocurrencies, and the Pepe meme became a symbol of the intersection between internet culture and blockchain technology.

Overall, the Rare Pepe Party represents an early example of the potential for memes and internet culture to be leveraged for financial gain through the use of blockchain technology. While the project faced its share of challenges, it also demonstrated the power of community and the ability of memes to capture the attention and imagination of a wide audience.

Counterparty's role in creating Rare Pepe Party

Counterparty is an open-source platform built on top of the Bitcoin blockchain that allows for the creation of custom tokens and smart contracts. It was launched in 2014 by a group of Bitcoin developers who believed that the blockchain could be used for more than just a payment system.

Counterparty uses the Bitcoin blockchain as its underlying technology, but it has its own set of rules and functions that allow for the creation of new assets and the execution of smart contracts. This means that users can create new tokens that represent anything from real-world assets to digital collectibles like Rare Pepe Party.

Counterparty's role in creating Rare Pepe Party is significant because it provided the platform for the creation, distribution, and trading of Rare Pepe Party tokens. The platform allowed users to create custom tokens that were linked to digital art and memes, which could then be traded on the Counterparty decentralized exchange.

The creators of Rare Pepe Party saw the potential of using Counterparty to create a unique token that represented digital art. The Rare Pepe Party tokens were created as a way to bring attention to the potential of digital collectibles on the blockchain. The Rare Pepe Party tokens were not just any token, they were unique tokens that were linked to a specific piece of digital art.

Counterparty's smart contract functionality allowed the creators of Rare Pepe Party to program certain behaviors into the tokens, such as limiting the number of tokens available or setting rules for how they could be traded. This added a layer of security and authenticity to the tokens that made them more valuable and desirable to collectors.

Rare Pepe Party was one of the first examples of using blockchain technology for the creation and distribution of digital collectibles, and it helped to pave the way for other projects in the space, such as CryptoKitties and NBA Top Shot.

In conclusion, Counterparty played a critical role in the creation of Rare Pepe Party by providing the platform for the creation, distribution, and trading of the tokens. The smart contract functionality of the platform allowed for the programming of specific behaviors into the tokens, which added a layer of security and authenticity that made them more valuable and desirable to collectors. The success of Rare Pepe Party helped to demonstrate the potential of digital collectibles on the blockchain and helped to pave the way for other similar projects.

The Pepe meme and its significance in meme culture

The Pepe meme is one of the most recognizable memes in internet culture, and it has gained widespread popularity in recent years. Its origins can be traced back to the comic book "Boy's Club," created by artist Matt Furie in 2005. The character of Pepe first appeared in the comic as a laid-back, stoner frog, and quickly became a hit with readers.

Over time, the character of Pepe began to evolve beyond its original comic book roots and take on a life of its own on the internet. In the early days of meme culture, Pepe was primarily used as a reaction image, often paired with humorous captions or used to convey emotions such as sadness or frustration.

As Pepe continued to grow in popularity, it began to take on a more subversive edge. The character became associated with various countercultural movements, such as the alt-right, and was co-opted by some as a symbol of hate and bigotry. However, it is important to note that the majority of Pepe's use is not associated with any negative connotations.

Despite its controversial associations, the Pepe meme remains one of the most recognizable and beloved memes in internet culture. It has spawned countless variations and spin-offs, including the Rare Pepe Party.

The significance of the Pepe meme in meme culture cannot be overstated. It represents the evolution of memes from simple reaction images to complex cultural artifacts with their own histories, meanings, and subcultures. The success of Rare Pepe Party and other meme coins is due in no small part to the power of the Pepe meme and its ability to capture the imagination of internet users around the world.

In many ways, the Pepe meme has become a symbol of the power and influence of meme culture. As meme coins continue to gain popularity and mainstream acceptance, it is likely that the Pepe meme and other popular internet memes will continue to play an important role in shaping the future of cryptocurrency and the wider cultural landscape.

The economics of Rare Pepe Party

Rare Pepe Party was one of the first successful projects built on top of the Counterparty platform. The project created a new kind of digital asset that was essentially a digital trading card featuring the popular Pepe meme. Each Rare Pepe card was unique, and the scarcity of each card was enforced by the blockchain. In order to acquire a Rare Pepe, users had to buy them on a decentralized exchange or trade them with other users.

The Rare Pepe Party project gained a significant following within the cryptocurrency community, particularly among those who were already familiar with the Pepe meme. The project's success can be attributed to several factors, including the uniqueness and scarcity of the assets, the community-driven nature of the project, and the growing interest in blockchain technology and cryptocurrencies.

One of the key features of Rare Pepe Party was the use of Counterparty tokens, which were used to represent each Rare Pepe card. Counterparty is a platform that allows developers to build custom financial instruments on top of the Bitcoin blockchain. This meant that Rare Pepe Party was able to take advantage of the security and transparency of the blockchain, while also benefiting from the flexibility and programmability of the Counterparty platform.

In terms of economics, Rare Pepe Party was an interesting experiment in creating a market for digital assets. Each Rare Pepe card was unique, and their scarcity was enforced by the blockchain. This created a situation where the value of each card was determined by supply and demand, just like a traditional physical trading card. However, because the market for Rare Pepe cards was entirely digital, it was able to operate on a global scale, with buyers and sellers from all over the world.

The value of Rare Pepe cards varied widely, with some cards selling for just a few dollars and others selling for tens of thousands of dollars. The most valuable cards were often those that were the most rare or the most popular among collectors. Some collectors even went so far as to create their own Rare Pepe cards and sell them on the market.

The Rare Pepe Party project also introduced a new concept in the world of digital assets: proof of ownership. Because each Rare Pepe card was unique, it was possible for collectors to prove that they owned a specific card by publishing its cryptographic signature on the blockchain. This made it possible to verify the authenticity of Rare Pepe cards and created a sense of trust within the community.

Overall, the Rare Pepe Party project was an interesting experiment in creating a market for digital assets.

It demonstrated the potential of blockchain technology to create new kinds of financial instruments and marketplaces. While the project was short-lived and its success was ultimately limited, it paved the way for future projects that would build on its innovative ideas.

The legacy of Rare Pepe Party in the crypto world

The Rare Pepe Party project may have been short-lived, but its impact on the crypto world cannot be denied. In this section, we will explore the legacy of Rare Pepe Party and its impact on the world of digital art and collectibles.

1. Pioneering the concept of rare digital art Rare Pepe Party was one of the first projects to explore the concept of rare digital art. By using blockchain technology, they were able to create unique digital assets that were verifiable and scarce, similar to traditional collectibles. This paved the way for other projects like CryptoKitties and CryptoPunks, which became immensely popular in the following years.

2. Introducing the concept of asset-backed tokens Rare Pepe Party also introduced the concept of asset-backed tokens, where the value of a token is tied to a physical asset. In the case of Rare Pepe Party, the tokens represented rare digital artwork. This concept has since been used in other projects, including those that allow users to invest in real estate or commodities through tokenization.

3. Inspiring the creation of other meme-based projects The success of Rare Pepe Party inspired the creation of other meme-based projects, including projects like MoonCats and Hashmasks. These projects also used

blockchain technology to create unique and rare digital assets based on popular memes.

4. Showcasing the potential of Counterparty Rare Pepe Party was built on the Counterparty platform, which showed the potential of this relatively unknown platform. Although Counterparty never became as popular as other blockchain platforms like Ethereum, it still has a dedicated community and is used in various projects.

5. Highlighting the potential of blockchain technology for the art world Finally, Rare Pepe Party highlighted the potential of blockchain technology for the art world. By creating unique digital assets that were verifiable and scarce, they showed that blockchain technology could revolutionize the art world by making it more accessible and transparent.

In conclusion, the Rare Pepe Party project may have been short-lived, but its impact on the crypto world was significant. By pioneering the concept of rare digital art and introducing the concept of asset-backed tokens, they paved the way for other popular projects. They also inspired the creation of other meme-based projects, highlighted the potential of Counterparty, and showcased the potential of blockchain technology for the art world.

Chapter 3: BBQCoin, Scrypt, launched in 2013, USD 1.1 million ATH in Dec 2013

History and origin of BBQCoin

BBQCoin was a short-lived cryptocurrency that was launched in 2013. The currency was based on the Scrypt algorithm and had a market capitalization of around $1.1 million at its peak in December 2013. BBQCoin was intended to be a fun and quirky cryptocurrency that could be used to purchase barbecue-related items and services. Despite its unique concept, the currency ultimately failed to gain widespread adoption and interest waned.

The origins of BBQCoin can be traced back to a post on the Bitcointalk forum in March 2013 by a user named "ribuck". In the post, ribuck proposed the idea of creating a new cryptocurrency called BBQCoin, which would be used to buy and sell barbecue-related goods and services. The post generated a lot of interest and soon a developer named "Luckycoiner" stepped forward to help create the currency.

BBQCoin was based on the Scrypt algorithm, which was designed to be more resistant to ASIC mining than the SHA-256 algorithm used by Bitcoin. The developers hoped that this would make it easier for users to mine the currency using their own computers, rather than having to purchase expensive mining hardware. The currency was also designed to have a faster block time than Bitcoin, with new blocks being created every 30 seconds.

Initially, BBQCoin was not taken very seriously by the wider cryptocurrency community. Many viewed it as a joke or a novelty currency, and there were concerns that it was simply a "pump and dump" scheme designed to enrich its creators. However, the currency did manage to attract a small following of enthusiasts who appreciated its lighthearted nature and unique concept.

One of the main selling points of BBQCoin was its low price. The currency was initially offered at a rate of 1000 BBQCoins per Bitcoin, which made it accessible to even the most casual of cryptocurrency enthusiasts. However, the currency's value quickly began to rise as more people became interested in it. By May 2013, the price of BBQCoin had risen to 50 BBQCoins per Bitcoin, and by December of that year it had peaked at around 1,000 BBQCoins per Bitcoin.

Despite its initial success, BBQCoin ultimately failed to gain widespread adoption. The currency was not widely accepted by merchants or exchanges, and many people remained skeptical of its long-term viability. In addition, the BBQCoin community was never able to develop the kind of passionate and dedicated following that helped to propel currencies like Dogecoin to success.

Today, BBQCoin is largely forgotten, and its market capitalization is a fraction of what it was at its peak. However, the currency's brief existence serves as a reminder of the potential that cryptocurrencies have to disrupt traditional financial systems and to inspire creativity and innovation in unexpected ways.

The technical features of BBQCoin

BBQCoin is a cryptocurrency that was launched in 2013, and it is based on the Scrypt algorithm. As such, it shares many similarities with other Scrypt-based cryptocurrencies, such as Litecoin and Dogecoin. However, there are also some unique technical features that set BBQCoin apart from other cryptocurrencies.

One of the main technical features of BBQCoin is its block time. BBQCoin has a block time of just one minute, which is faster than most other cryptocurrencies. This means that transactions can be confirmed more quickly, and users can send and receive funds more rapidly. However, this fast block time also has some drawbacks. For example, it can lead to an increased likelihood of orphaned blocks and blockchain forks, which can create problems for users and miners.

Another technical feature of BBQCoin is its block reward. Like many cryptocurrencies, BBQCoin uses a proof-of-work consensus algorithm to secure its network and validate transactions. Miners who successfully solve blocks are rewarded with newly minted BBQCoins. In the case of BBQCoin, the block reward starts at 5000 coins per block and is halved every 50,000 blocks. This means that the total supply of BBQCoin is limited, which can help to prevent inflation and maintain the value of the currency.

BBQCoin also uses a different hashing algorithm than other Scrypt-based cryptocurrencies. While most Scrypt-based coins use Scrypt-N or Scrypt-jane, BBQCoin uses a modified version of Scrypt that is specifically designed for BBQCoin. This modification allows for more efficient mining and greater hash power, which can make the network more secure and reduce the likelihood of 51% attacks.

Finally, BBQCoin has some unique features that are specific to its use case. For example, BBQCoin was originally designed as a payment system for BBQ restaurants and other food-related businesses. As such, it includes features like a built-in tipping system, which allows customers to tip their servers or chefs with BBQCoins. It also includes a loyalty program, which rewards frequent customers with additional coins or discounts.

In conclusion, BBQCoin has several unique technical features that set it apart from other cryptocurrencies. Its fast block time, limited supply, and modified Scrypt algorithm make it a unique and efficient payment system. Additionally, its specific use case as a currency for BBQ restaurants and food-related businesses gives it a niche appeal and loyal user base.

The use cases and real-world adoption of BBQCoin

BBQCoin is a cryptocurrency that has been around since 2013. It is a Scrypt-based coin that was designed to be a fun and lighthearted alternative to the more serious cryptocurrencies. BBQCoin has never gained the same level of popularity as Dogecoin or some other meme coins, but it does have a small but dedicated following.

Use Cases of BBQCoin

BBQCoin has had limited real-world adoption, but there have been a few cases where it has been used for transactions. Some businesses have accepted BBQCoin as a form of payment, including a few online stores that sell barbeque-related products. However, these businesses are few and far between, and it is not common to find places that accept BBQCoin.

Another use case for BBQCoin is as a speculative investment. Like many other cryptocurrencies, the price of BBQCoin is highly volatile, and there is potential for investors to make a significant profit if they buy at the right time and sell when the price is high. However, this is a risky strategy, as the price of BBQCoin can also plummet just as quickly as it rises.

BBQCoin also has some practical use cases. One of the features of BBQCoin is its fast transaction processing time.

Transactions are processed quickly, making it an attractive option for those who need to send or receive money quickly. Additionally, the low transaction fees associated with BBQCoin make it an appealing choice for those who want to transfer funds without having to pay high fees.

Real-world Adoption of BBQCoin

Despite its limited real-world adoption, there have been a few instances where BBQCoin has been used in transactions. In 2013, a Reddit user posted that they had purchased a hamburger with BBQCoin. The post was widely shared in the cryptocurrency community and helped to bring some attention to BBQCoin.

Since then, there have been a few other instances where BBQCoin has been used as a form of payment. In 2014, a website called BBQCoinFaucet was launched, which allowed users to earn BBQCoin by completing simple tasks. Users could then use the BBQCoin they earned to purchase various items, including physical barbeque-related products.

In 2015, a Reddit user posted that they had used BBQCoin to purchase a barbeque smoker. The post received some attention, and other users expressed interest in using BBQCoin for similar transactions. However, there has not been much activity surrounding BBQCoin since then, and it remains a relatively obscure cryptocurrency.

Challenges to Adoption

One of the main challenges to adoption for BBQCoin is its lack of mainstream recognition. While some cryptocurrency enthusiasts are aware of BBQCoin, it is not well-known outside of this niche community. This makes it difficult to convince businesses to accept BBQCoin as a form of payment.

Another challenge to adoption is the limited number of use cases for BBQCoin. While it has some practical use cases, such as its fast transaction processing time and low fees, there are many other cryptocurrencies that offer similar features. Additionally, the lack of mainstream adoption means that there are few places where BBQCoin can be used for transactions.

Finally, the high volatility of the price of BBQCoin is a significant obstacle to adoption. While there is potential for investors to make a significant profit by buying and selling BBQCoin at the right time, the high risk associated with this strategy means that many people are hesitant to invest in BBQCoin.

Conclusion

BBQCoin is a Scrypt-based cryptocurrency that was launched in 2013. While it has some practical use cases, such as its fast transaction processing time and low fees, it has not gained widespread adoption. Its lack of mainstream recognition, limited use cases, and high volatility have all contributed to its relatively low profile in the cryptocurrency world. Despite this, there is still a small but dedicated community of BBQCoin enthusiasts who continue to mine and trade the coin, and some have even developed unique use cases for it, such as in the world of online gaming.

Overall, BBQCoin's technical features make it a fast and efficient cryptocurrency with potential for niche use cases. However, its limited adoption and high volatility mean that it is not currently a major player in the wider cryptocurrency market. As the crypto landscape continues to evolve, it remains to be seen if BBQCoin will see increased adoption and recognition or if it will remain a niche coin with a devoted following.

BBQCoin's rise and fall in the crypto market

BBQCoin is a Scrypt-based cryptocurrency that was launched in 2013 as a tongue-in-cheek alternative to Bitcoin. Despite its seemingly unserious nature, it managed to achieve a market capitalization of over $1 million in December 2013, shortly after its launch. However, the currency's value quickly declined, and it never reached the heights of Bitcoin or other cryptocurrencies. In this section, we will explore the rise and fall of BBQCoin in the crypto market.

BBQCoin was initially greeted with skepticism by many in the crypto community due to its whimsical nature. However, it quickly gained a following among those who appreciated its lightheartedness and wanted to support a coin that wasn't solely focused on profit. The community behind BBQCoin was small but dedicated, and they worked hard to promote the coin and its features.

One of the main selling points of BBQCoin was its fast transaction processing time and low fees, which made it an attractive option for those who wanted to transfer funds quickly and cheaply. Additionally, the coin's algorithm was designed to ensure a fair distribution of coins, which made it more accessible to those who wanted to mine it.

Despite its early success, BBQCoin's market capitalization began to decline rapidly in early 2014. This was due to a combination of factors, including a lack of mainstream recognition, limited use cases, and high volatility. The coin's value was also heavily dependent on the overall state of the cryptocurrency market, which was experiencing a downturn at the time.

As interest in BBQCoin waned, the community behind it also began to lose momentum. Development on the coin slowed, and fewer people were actively mining or using it. By the end of 2014, its market capitalization had dropped to less than $100,000, and it continued to decline in the years that followed.

Despite its decline, BBQCoin still has a small but dedicated community of supporters who continue to believe in its potential. Some see it as a novelty coin that has a place in the crypto world alongside other more serious cryptocurrencies, while others see it as a potential investment opportunity.

In recent years, BBQCoin's market capitalization has remained relatively stable, hovering around $20,000 to $30,000. While this is a far cry from its peak in 2013, it shows that there is still some interest in the coin. However, it is unlikely that BBQCoin will ever achieve the same level of success that it did in its early days, given the competitive nature of the cryptocurrency market and the many other options available to investors.

In conclusion, BBQCoin's rise and fall in the crypto market is a cautionary tale about the unpredictable nature of the cryptocurrency world. Despite its early success and dedicated community, the coin was unable to maintain its momentum due to a combination of factors. While it may still have some value as a novelty coin or investment opportunity, its limited use cases and lack of mainstream recognition make it a risky choice for most investors.

Lessons learned from BBQCoin's experience

BBQCoin's rise and fall in the cryptocurrency market provides valuable lessons that can be learned by investors, developers, and enthusiasts in the industry. Here are some of the key takeaways from the BBQCoin experience:

1. Avoid Pump-and-Dump Schemes: BBQCoin's ATH in 2013 was largely driven by a pump-and-dump scheme orchestrated by a group of traders. Investors should be wary of cryptocurrencies that experience sudden and unnatural price increases, as they are often the result of manipulation rather than genuine market demand.

2. Real-world Adoption is Key: While BBQCoin had some practical use cases, such as its fast transaction processing time and low fees, it failed to gain widespread adoption. This highlights the importance of real-world use cases for cryptocurrencies, as without them, they may struggle to gain mainstream recognition.

3. Be Prepared for Volatility: BBQCoin's price was highly volatile, with significant fluctuations in a short amount of time. This is a common feature of many cryptocurrencies, and investors should be aware of the risks associated with investing in assets with high volatility.

4. Community is Important: The success of a cryptocurrency is often closely tied to its community.

BBQCoin's community was relatively small and inactive, which may have contributed to its lack of adoption and eventual decline.

5. Innovation is Key: The cryptocurrency market is constantly evolving, and successful cryptocurrencies often have innovative features that differentiate them from others. BBQCoin, on the other hand, was largely a clone of Litecoin, with few distinguishing features.

6. Learn from Mistakes: BBQCoin's developers made some mistakes, such as failing to update the software and address security vulnerabilities. It's important for developers to learn from their mistakes and continually improve their projects to avoid similar issues in the future.

In conclusion, BBQCoin's experience provides a valuable case study for anyone interested in the cryptocurrency industry. By understanding the lessons learned from BBQCoin's rise and fall, investors, developers, and enthusiasts can make more informed decisions and build stronger, more successful projects.

Chapter 4: NyanCoin, Scrypt, launched in 2014, USD 1 million ATH in Jan 2014

History and origin of NyanCoin

NyanCoin is a digital currency that was launched in early 2014. It is based on the Scrypt algorithm and was created as a humorous alternative to other cryptocurrencies like Bitcoin and Litecoin. The currency was named after the popular internet meme Nyan Cat, which features a cartoon cat with a Pop-Tart body flying through space leaving a rainbow trail behind it. The idea behind NyanCoin was to create a fun and light-hearted cryptocurrency that would appeal to a wider audience.

The NyanCoin project was started by a developer who goes by the pseudonym "NyanKitten". According to NyanKitten, the idea for NyanCoin came about after he saw the success of Dogecoin, another meme-based cryptocurrency. He believed that a currency based on the popular Nyan Cat meme could also be successful.

The NyanCoin network was launched on January 7th, 2014, with an initial block reward of 337 NYAN per block. The currency gained popularity quickly, with its value peaking at $1 million in market capitalization just a few weeks after its launch. However, the currency's value would ultimately drop significantly in the following months.

Despite its relative lack of adoption, NyanCoin has remained an important part of cryptocurrency history, thanks in part to its unique branding and the internet meme that inspired it. The currency has also served as an example of the potential for humorous and lighthearted cryptocurrencies to gain traction in the market.

The technical features of NyanCoin

NyanCoin, like many cryptocurrencies, is based on the Scrypt algorithm, which is designed to be memory-hard and resistant to ASIC mining. However, NyanCoin also incorporates a few unique technical features that set it apart from other Scrypt-based coins.

One of these features is its mining algorithm, which uses the Kimoto Gravity Well (KGW) to adjust the difficulty of mining. This algorithm adjusts the difficulty of mining based on the rate at which new blocks are being generated, which helps to prevent large miners from dominating the network and destabilizing the coin's value.

Another unique feature of NyanCoin is its use of the "nyan" meme as its branding and marketing strategy. The coin's official website and social media channels are filled with references to cats, rainbows, and other cute and colorful imagery associated with the meme.

NyanCoin also has a relatively fast block time of 1 minute, which allows for quick transaction confirmations and ensures that the network can handle a high volume of transactions.

Additionally, NyanCoin has a fixed maximum supply of 337 million coins, which is intended to prevent inflation and ensure that the coin maintains its value over time.

Overall, while NyanCoin's technical features are not revolutionary, they do help to differentiate the coin from other Scrypt-based cryptocurrencies and have contributed to its popularity among certain segments of the crypto community.

NyanCoin's use cases and real-world adoption

NyanCoin, like many cryptocurrencies, was created with the intention of providing a fast, secure, and decentralized means of value transfer. However, despite its unique branding and active community, NyanCoin has struggled to gain widespread adoption outside of the cryptocurrency space.

One of the primary use cases for NyanCoin has been as a means of tipping or rewarding content creators online. NyanCoin's fun and whimsical branding, along with its fast transaction processing time and low fees, have made it popular among some online communities. For example, the NyanCoin community has been known to tip creators on platforms like Reddit and Twitch using the cryptocurrency.

Another potential use case for NyanCoin is as a store of value or investment. NyanCoin's relatively low supply, combined with its active community and unique branding, have made it attractive to some investors looking for alternatives to more well-known cryptocurrencies like Bitcoin and Ethereum.

However, despite these potential use cases, NyanCoin has not seen significant adoption outside of the cryptocurrency space. While the NyanCoin community is active and engaged, it remains relatively small compared to other cryptocurrencies. This lack of mainstream adoption has limited the potential for NyanCoin to be used as a means of payment or transfer in the real world.

There have been some attempts to increase NyanCoin's real-world adoption, such as partnerships with online stores and businesses that accept the cryptocurrency as payment. However, these efforts have been limited in scope and have not led to significant increases in adoption.

Overall, while NyanCoin has some unique features and potential use cases, it has struggled to gain significant real-world adoption. The cryptocurrency's primary appeal has been to its dedicated community of users and investors, rather than to a wider audience outside of the cryptocurrency space.

NyanCoin's rise and fall in the crypto market

NyanCoin was launched in early 2014 and quickly gained popularity in the cryptocurrency community. Its cute and playful branding, coupled with its unique features, made it an attractive investment for many crypto enthusiasts. NyanCoin's price reached an all-time high of $1 million in January 2014, but the price soon plummeted, and the coin lost most of its value.

One of the reasons for NyanCoin's rapid rise and fall was its lack of real-world use cases. While some merchants accepted NyanCoin as a payment method, it was not widely adopted as a means of payment. Additionally, the coin was primarily used for speculative purposes, and many investors bought it solely because they believed its price would continue to rise.

Another factor that contributed to NyanCoin's decline was the emergence of newer and more advanced cryptocurrencies. As the cryptocurrency market became more competitive, NyanCoin lost its appeal to investors who were looking for more advanced technology and more robust use cases.

Furthermore, NyanCoin was also a victim of the broader cryptocurrency market's downturn. In 2014, the cryptocurrency market experienced a significant price drop, and many coins, including NyanCoin, lost most of their value. As investors began to lose confidence in the market, they started selling their coins, causing a further decline in prices.

NyanCoin's fall in value was also due to its lack of development and community support. Despite being a popular coin, NyanCoin's developers did not actively work on the project, and the community support was not strong enough to sustain the coin's growth. As a result, NyanCoin was left behind in the cryptocurrency race, and its popularity and value declined.

In conclusion, NyanCoin's rise and fall in the crypto market was a combination of several factors. Its lack of real-world use cases, the emergence of newer and more advanced cryptocurrencies, the broader cryptocurrency market's downturn, and the lack of development and community support all contributed to its decline. NyanCoin's story serves as a cautionary tale for cryptocurrency investors, highlighting the importance of thorough research and analysis before investing in any coin.

Lessons learned from NyanCoin's experience

NyanCoin was a cryptocurrency that experienced a meteoric rise and fall in the cryptocurrency market. Its story serves as a cautionary tale for investors and developers alike, highlighting the importance of careful planning, community engagement, and a long-term vision for the project's success. In this section, we will examine the key lessons that can be learned from NyanCoin's experience.

1. Community engagement is crucial

One of the key factors behind NyanCoin's success was its vibrant and engaged community. The project's developers were active in online forums such as Reddit and Bitcointalk, answering questions and soliciting feedback from users. This community support helped to build a sense of trust and enthusiasm around the project, which in turn drove up demand for the currency.

However, when the original developers left the project, the community was left without clear leadership or direction. This led to a loss of momentum and a decline in interest in the currency, ultimately contributing to its downfall. The lesson here is clear: community engagement is crucial for the success of any cryptocurrency project, and developers must work to maintain and cultivate a strong and dedicated user base.

2. Plan for the long term

NyanCoin's initial success was driven largely by hype and speculation. However, the project lacked a clear long-term plan for development and adoption. As a result, when interest in the currency waned, there was little to keep it afloat.

Developers must plan for the long term, considering factors such as scalability, security, and real-world use cases. They must also have a clear vision for the project's future, including a roadmap for development and a strategy for community engagement and adoption.

3. Beware of pump-and-dump schemes

NyanCoin was the victim of several pump-and-dump schemes, in which groups of investors artificially drove up the price of the currency before quickly selling their holdings and leaving other investors with worthless coins. These schemes can be difficult to detect, but investors must be wary of projects that experience sudden and inexplicable spikes in price.

4. Technical competence is essential

NyanCoin was based on the Scrypt algorithm, which is commonly used in cryptocurrency mining. However, the project's code was poorly written and contained numerous bugs and vulnerabilities. This lack of technical competence ultimately contributed to the project's downfall, as users lost faith in its security and stability.

Developers must prioritize technical competence, ensuring that their code is well-written, well-documented, and thoroughly tested. They must also stay up to date on the latest developments in the field, including new technologies and security threats.

5. Don't ignore regulatory concerns

Finally, NyanCoin's developers and investors largely ignored regulatory concerns, operating in a legal grey area that ultimately made the project vulnerable to legal action. While cryptocurrency regulation remains a complex and evolving field, developers must be aware of the legal risks associated with their projects and take steps to mitigate those risks.

In conclusion, NyanCoin's rise and fall provide a valuable set of lessons for cryptocurrency investors and developers alike. By engaging with their communities, planning for the long term, avoiding pump-and-dump schemes, prioritizing technical competence, and being mindful of regulatory concerns, developers can create projects that are stable, sustainable, and successful in the long run.

Chapter 5: HoboNickels, Scrypt, launched in 2013, USD 0.2 million ATH in Dec 2013

History and origin of HoboNickels

HoboNickels is a Scrypt-based cryptocurrency that was launched in 2013. It was created by a developer who used the pseudonym "Tranz" and was initially called "HoboNickels for the Homeless." The project aimed to raise awareness and funds for homeless individuals, as a portion of the coins mined were donated to charity organizations that helped the homeless. The idea behind the project was to create a cryptocurrency that not only provided a secure and decentralized way of making transactions but also had a social impact.

The name "HoboNickels" was inspired by a form of currency used by the homeless during the Great Depression in the United States. Hobos would carve their own nickels from discarded materials, such as tin cans, as a way of creating their own currency. The name also reflects the project's original purpose of supporting the homeless.

HoboNickels initially used the Proof of Work (PoW) consensus mechanism and had a total supply of 84 million coins. The initial block reward was 100 coins, which was halved every 1 million blocks. The block time was 120 seconds, and the difficulty adjustment algorithm used was the Dark Gravity Wave v3. The project had a small community of enthusiasts who supported the cause and helped spread the word about the project.

In 2014, the HoboNickels project experienced a major setback when Tranz announced that he would no longer be actively working on the project due to personal reasons. The community was left without a lead developer, and the project went into a state of uncertainty. However, a few community members stepped up to take over the development and maintenance of the project.

Under the new leadership, the HoboNickels project underwent several changes and improvements. In 2015, the project switched to a hybrid consensus mechanism, combining PoW and Proof of Stake (PoS). This change allowed users to earn new coins by holding their existing coins in a wallet and participating in the network's validation process.

The new team also implemented several technical improvements to the project, including faster block times and a new difficulty algorithm. They also focused on expanding the project's reach and increasing its adoption. They worked on getting HoboNickels listed on various cryptocurrency exchanges and partnered with merchants to accept HoboNickels as a payment method.

Today, HoboNickels is still active, and its community is continuously working on improving and expanding the project. The project has come a long way since its early days, and its original purpose of supporting the homeless has evolved into a broader goal of promoting social impact through the use of cryptocurrency.

In conclusion, HoboNickels is a unique cryptocurrency project that aimed to support the homeless community while providing a secure and decentralized way of making transactions. The project faced several challenges, including the departure of its lead developer, but managed to overcome them and continue growing under the leadership of its dedicated community. The project's name and original purpose serve as a reminder of the potential of cryptocurrency to not only revolutionize the financial industry but also have a positive impact on society.

The technical features of HoboNickels

HoboNickels is a Scrypt-based cryptocurrency that was launched in 2013. It was created as a fork of the popular Litecoin cryptocurrency with several technical improvements. Some of the technical features of HoboNickels include:

1. Block Time: The block time of HoboNickels is set at 120 seconds, which is twice as fast as the block time of Litecoin. This means that transactions can be confirmed faster on the HoboNickels network.

2. Proof-of-Stake: HoboNickels uses a hybrid proof-of-work and proof-of-stake consensus mechanism. Proof-of-stake is used to secure the network and generate new blocks. This means that users who hold HoboNickels can participate in the network's security and earn rewards for doing so.

3. Advanced Encryption: HoboNickels uses advanced encryption algorithms to secure transactions and protect the privacy of users. It also has an optional feature called "Stealth Addresses" that allows users to make transactions without revealing their public addresses.

4. Difficulty Adjustment: HoboNickels has an adaptive difficulty adjustment algorithm that ensures that the block time remains consistent even as the network hash

rate changes. This helps to prevent large fluctuations in block time and makes the network more stable.

5. Multi-Platform Support: HoboNickels is supported on multiple platforms, including Windows, Linux, and macOS. This makes it accessible to a wider range of users and helps to increase adoption.

6. Open-Source: HoboNickels is an open-source project, which means that the source code is freely available to anyone who wants to contribute to the project or build on top of it.

Overall, the technical features of HoboNickels make it a fast, secure, and accessible cryptocurrency that is well-suited for everyday use. Its proof-of-stake mechanism also incentivizes users to hold and use the currency, which can help to drive adoption and increase its value over time.

HoboNickels' use cases and real-world adoption

HoboNickels (HBN) is a Scrypt-based cryptocurrency that was launched in 2013. It was designed to be a fast, secure, and reliable digital currency that could be used for a wide range of purposes. Despite its many technical advantages, HoboNickels has not been widely adopted in the real world. In this section, we will explore the various use cases and real-world adoption of HoboNickels.

One of the most promising use cases for HoboNickels is as a means of payment for online purchases. The cryptocurrency's fast transaction processing time and low fees make it an attractive alternative to traditional payment methods like credit cards and PayPal. Several online retailers and service providers have already begun accepting HoboNickels as payment, including VPN providers and web hosting companies. However, the overall number of merchants accepting HoboNickels remains relatively low, which limits its usefulness as a payment method.

Another potential use case for HoboNickels is as a store of value. Cryptocurrencies have gained a reputation as a highly speculative investment, and many people have invested in them as a way to make quick profits. However, this has also led to significant price volatility, which can make it difficult to hold cryptocurrencies as a long-term investment. HoboNickels' low inflation rate and stable price could make it an attractive investment option for those looking to hold onto their wealth for an extended period.

HoboNickels can also be used as a means of remittance. Cross-border transactions are often slow, expensive, and unreliable, especially when traditional financial institutions are involved. HoboNickels can be sent anywhere in the world quickly and cheaply, making it an attractive option for people who need to send money overseas. Additionally, HoboNickels can be used to bypass capital controls, which are often used by authoritarian governments to restrict the movement of funds.

One of the more unique use cases for HoboNickels is as a tool for charity. The HoboNickels community has a long history of supporting various charitable causes, such as disaster relief efforts and community development projects. Charities can accept donations in HoboNickels, which can then be used to fund various programs and initiatives. This is a relatively new use case for cryptocurrencies, but it has the potential to become a significant source of funding for charitable organizations.

Despite its many potential use cases, HoboNickels has not seen widespread adoption in the real world. The cryptocurrency remains relatively unknown outside of the cryptocurrency community, which limits its usefulness as a means of payment and store of value. Additionally, many of the merchants and service providers that accept HoboNickels are themselves relatively small and unknown, which can make it difficult for users to find opportunities to spend their cryptocurrency.

In conclusion, HoboNickels has several potential use cases in the real world, including as a means of payment, store of value, remittance, and tool for charity. However, the cryptocurrency's limited adoption and lack of recognition outside of the cryptocurrency community have hampered its growth and development. Nevertheless, as the cryptocurrency market continues to mature, there may be new opportunities for HoboNickels to gain wider acceptance and adoption.

HoboNickels' rise and fall in the crypto market

HoboNickels (HBN) is a Scrypt-based cryptocurrency that was launched in July 2013. While it enjoyed a brief period of success, it has since faded into obscurity. In this section, we will explore the factors that led to HoboNickels' rise and fall in the cryptocurrency market.

Launch and Initial Success

HoboNickels was launched in July 2013 by a developer known as "Tranz" on the Bitcointalk forum. It was designed as a Scrypt-based cryptocurrency with a maximum supply of 100 million coins. The coin's name and logo were inspired by the lifestyle of hobos and the imagery associated with the Great Depression.

The coin quickly gained popularity within the cryptocurrency community, and its value rose steadily in the months following its launch. In December 2013, HoboNickels reached its all-time high of $0.0237 USD. This was a significant achievement for a coin that had only been in existence for a few months.

However, HoboNickels' success was short-lived, and its value began to decline rapidly in early 2014. By the end of the year, its value had dropped to less than $0.001 USD.

Factors Contributing to HoboNickels' Decline

There were several factors that contributed to HoboNickels' decline in the cryptocurrency market. One of the most significant factors was the coin's lack of innovation. While HoboNickels was initially popular due to its unique branding and community, it failed to offer any significant technical advancements compared to other cryptocurrencies.

HoboNickels' development was also slow, with only a few updates being released in the years following its launch. This lack of development led to a decline in interest from both users and investors.

Furthermore, HoboNickels faced several technical issues that hindered its adoption. One of the most notable issues was a bug in the coin's code that allowed for the creation of fake transactions. This flaw made the coin vulnerable to attack, and it was eventually exploited by hackers who used it to create large amounts of fake HBN transactions.

Another factor that contributed to HoboNickels' decline was the overall market trend. In 2014, the cryptocurrency market experienced a significant downturn, with many coins losing value. HoboNickels was no exception and saw a significant drop in value during this period.

Lessons Learned from HoboNickels' Experience

The rise and fall of HoboNickels highlight several lessons that can be learned by cryptocurrency developers and investors. One of the most important lessons is the importance of innovation. In a market as competitive as the cryptocurrency market, it is essential to offer something unique and valuable to users and investors.

Another critical lesson is the importance of ongoing development and maintenance. Cryptocurrencies require regular updates to fix bugs, improve performance, and introduce new features. Neglecting this aspect of cryptocurrency development can lead to a decline in interest and value.

Lastly, HoboNickels' experience highlights the importance of security in cryptocurrency development. Flaws in a coin's code can lead to significant problems, such as the creation of fake transactions, which can harm a coin's reputation and value.

In conclusion, while HoboNickels enjoyed a brief period of success, it ultimately failed to sustain its momentum due to a lack of innovation, slow development, and technical issues. The rise and fall of HoboNickels serve as a cautionary tale for cryptocurrency developers and investors, emphasizing the importance of innovation, ongoing development, and security in the cryptocurrency market.

Lessons learned from HoboNickels' experience

HoboNickels, like many other cryptocurrencies that emerged in the early days of the crypto market, experienced both highs and lows in terms of its value and adoption. There are several key lessons that can be learned from the rise and fall of HoboNickels.

1. Community is key

One of the most important factors in the success or failure of a cryptocurrency is the strength and engagement of its community. HoboNickels had a dedicated following of users who were passionate about the project and worked to improve it. However, as the market evolved and new cryptocurrencies emerged, some of the HoboNickels community members moved on to other projects, and the community became less active. This lack of engagement likely contributed to the decline in HoboNickels' value and adoption.

2. Innovation is necessary

In order to remain competitive in the cryptocurrency market, projects need to innovate and offer unique features and use cases. While HoboNickels had some innovative features when it was launched, such as its variable interest rate and support for advanced scripting, it did not continue to innovate and develop new features at the same pace as other projects. This lack of innovation may have contributed to the decline in HoboNickels' adoption and value.

3. Market volatility can be unpredictable

Like all cryptocurrencies, HoboNickels was subject to the volatility of the crypto market. While the project experienced a significant increase in value in 2013, it also saw a steep decline in 2014. The unpredictable nature of the market makes it difficult to predict the long-term success or failure of any cryptocurrency project.

4. Real-world adoption is key to success

Cryptocurrencies are ultimately only as valuable as their real-world adoption. While HoboNickels had some practical use cases, such as its fast transaction processing times and low fees, it did not gain widespread adoption in the same way as some other cryptocurrencies. This limited real-world adoption likely contributed to the decline in HoboNickels' value and popularity.

5. Communication is important

Effective communication with the community and potential investors is important for any cryptocurrency project. While HoboNickels had an active community at one point, the developers did not always effectively communicate with them or provide regular updates on the project's progress. This lack of communication may have contributed to a loss of confidence in the project and contributed to its decline.

6. Timing is everything

The timing of a cryptocurrency's launch can have a significant impact on its success or failure. HoboNickels was launched in 2013, a time when the crypto market was still relatively small and many people were just beginning to become interested in cryptocurrencies. However, as the market grew and became more crowded, HoboNickels struggled to compete with newer, more innovative projects.

In conclusion, the experience of HoboNickels highlights the challenges and opportunities that are inherent in the world of cryptocurrency. While the project had some innovative features and a dedicated community at one point, it ultimately struggled to maintain its momentum and compete with newer, more innovative projects. The lessons learned from the rise and fall of HoboNickels can help inform the development and success of future cryptocurrency projects.

Conclusion
The lasting impact of meme coins in the crypto world

Meme coins, a type of cryptocurrency that is often created as a joke or for fun, have left a lasting impact on the crypto world. While many of these coins have failed to gain widespread adoption or maintain their value, they have contributed to the development and evolution of the cryptocurrency space.

One of the most significant impacts of meme coins is their role in introducing new people to the world of cryptocurrencies. Memes have a wide reach and often go viral on social media platforms, allowing meme coins to reach a large audience and bring attention to the broader crypto ecosystem. Many people who were previously unaware of cryptocurrencies or were hesitant to invest have been drawn in by the humor and novelty of meme coins, leading them to explore other aspects of the crypto world.

Additionally, meme coins have pushed the boundaries of what is possible in the crypto world. These coins often feature unique and unconventional technical features or use cases, which have sparked innovation and experimentation among developers and crypto enthusiasts. For example, Dogecoin's use of the Scrypt algorithm, initially intended for

CPU mining, helped pave the way for the development of new mining algorithms and hardware.

Moreover, meme coins have also served as a form of commentary on the crypto industry itself. Many meme coins are created as a critique of traditional cryptocurrencies, highlighting issues such as high fees, slow transaction times, and a lack of accessibility for the average person. By poking fun at these issues and offering alternative solutions, meme coins have spurred important conversations and led to improvements in the crypto space.

However, it is important to note that meme coins also have their downsides. They can be highly volatile, with prices rising and falling rapidly based on social media trends and hype. This can make them risky investments for those who are not experienced in the crypto market. Additionally, the popularity of meme coins has led to the proliferation of scams and fraudulent coins, which can be difficult for investors to distinguish from legitimate projects.

Despite these challenges, meme coins have had a lasting impact on the crypto world, and their legacy is likely to continue for years to come. They have inspired new generations of crypto enthusiasts, challenged traditional notions of what a cryptocurrency can be, and contributed to the ongoing evolution of the industry. While not every meme coin may succeed, the lasting impact of these coins cannot be denied.

The challenges and opportunities of investing in meme coin

The world of cryptocurrency has seen an explosion of new projects and innovations over the last decade, and one of the most interesting phenomena to emerge from this ecosystem is the rise of meme coins. These are cryptocurrencies that are created with a humorous or satirical intent, often based on internet memes or pop culture references. Despite their often frivolous origins, meme coins have captured the attention of investors and the public alike, with some of them achieving remarkable success.

In this chapter, we will explore the challenges and opportunities of investing in meme coins. We will start by examining the risks and challenges that investors should be aware of when considering a meme coin investment. We will then discuss the potential benefits and opportunities that these investments can offer, including the possibility of high returns and the potential for a vibrant and engaged community.

One of the main challenges of investing in meme coins is the lack of fundamental value. Unlike traditional investments, which are typically based on underlying assets, earnings potential, or other fundamental factors, the value of meme coins is largely derived from market sentiment and community engagement. This means that meme coins can be subject to significant volatility and price fluctuations, making them a risky investment proposition.

Another challenge of investing in meme coins is the lack of regulation and oversight. Many meme coins are launched without the same level of scrutiny and oversight that traditional investments receive, which can make it difficult for investors to assess their risks and potential rewards. Additionally, meme coins are often the target of scams and frauds, with unscrupulous actors taking advantage of the hype and excitement surrounding these investments to defraud investors.

Despite these challenges, there are also significant opportunities for investors who are willing to take on the risks of meme coin investing. One of the main benefits of meme coins is the potential for high returns. Because these investments are often driven by hype and excitement, meme coins can experience significant price increases in a short period of time, leading to substantial profits for early investors.

Another benefit of meme coin investing is the potential for community engagement. Many meme coins have passionate and engaged communities that are active on social media and other platforms. This can create a sense of community and shared purpose that can be appealing to investors looking for a sense of belonging and engagement.

Finally, meme coins can also offer a unique opportunity for investors to participate in a new and rapidly evolving ecosystem. The world of cryptocurrency is constantly evolving, with new projects and innovations emerging all the time. By investing in meme coins, investors can be at the forefront of this rapidly changing landscape, with the potential to reap significant rewards as new opportunities emerge.

In conclusion, investing in meme coins can be a high-risk, high-reward proposition. These investments can offer the potential for significant profits and community engagement, but they also come with significant risks and challenges. As with any investment, it is important for investors to carefully evaluate the risks and potential rewards before making a decision. By doing so, investors can position themselves to take advantage of the unique opportunities and challenges presented by the world of meme coins and the wider cryptocurrency ecosystem.

The future of meme coins in the crypto landscape

Meme coins have made a significant impact on the crypto world, but what does the future hold for these digital assets? In this section, we will explore the future of meme coins and their potential impact on the crypto landscape.

1. Evolution of Meme Coins Meme coins have come a long way since the days of Dogecoin. As we have seen, many meme coins have incorporated advanced technical features and use cases that have enabled them to compete with more established cryptocurrencies. However, as meme coins continue to evolve, we may see even more innovative ideas and features implemented that will further increase their appeal.

2. Mainstream Adoption Despite their origins as a joke or parody, meme coins are slowly gaining mainstream recognition and adoption. This is largely due to their growing popularity and use cases, which are attracting more investors and businesses. As meme coins continue to prove their usefulness and value, we may see more widespread adoption of these digital assets in the future.

3. Increased Regulation As meme coins continue to gain popularity and value, it is likely that they will attract the attention of regulators. This could lead to increased scrutiny and regulation of meme coins, which could impact their

growth and adoption. However, it could also help to provide a more stable and secure environment for investors.

4. Increased Competition As the popularity of meme coins continues to grow, we may see increased competition from other cryptocurrencies and digital assets. This could lead to greater innovation and development in the space, but it could also lead to a consolidation of the market as investors gravitate towards more established cryptocurrencies.

5. Community-driven Development One of the defining characteristics of meme coins is their strong communities of supporters and developers. This community-driven approach has been key to the success of many meme coins, and we can expect it to continue to drive development and innovation in the space. As long as meme coins remain a community-driven endeavor, they will continue to offer unique and innovative ideas that could shape the future of the crypto landscape.

6. Potential Risks Despite their potential, investing in meme coins still carries a significant degree of risk. As we have seen with the rise and fall of various meme coins, the market can be volatile and unpredictable. It is important for investors to do their research and understand the risks

involved before investing in any digital asset, including meme coins.

Conclusion

In conclusion, meme coins have become an important part of the crypto landscape, offering unique and innovative ideas that have challenged established cryptocurrencies. While investing in meme coins carries significant risk, the potential rewards and opportunities are also significant. As meme coins continue to evolve and gain mainstream adoption, we can expect them to continue to shape the future of the crypto world. It is important for investors to stay informed and up-to-date on developments in the space, as well as to exercise caution and do their research before investing in any digital asset.

THE END

Key Terms and Definitions

To help you better understand the language and concepts related to aging and older adults, below you will find a list of key terms and their definitions.

1. Cryptocurrency - a digital or virtual currency that uses cryptography for security and operates independently of a central bank.

2. Meme - an image, video, or piece of text that is humorous in nature and spreads rapidly via the internet, often with variations or modifications.

3. Altcoin - any cryptocurrency other than Bitcoin.

4. Blockchain - a digital ledger of all cryptocurrency transactions that is distributed across a network of computers.

5. Proof-of-work - a consensus algorithm used by some cryptocurrencies, where miners compete to solve complex mathematical problems to validate transactions and earn rewards.

6. Scrypt - a key derivation function used by some cryptocurrencies, designed to be more memory-intensive than SHA-256 (used by Bitcoin) and therefore more resistant to ASIC mining.

7. ATH (All-time high) - the highest price level that a cryptocurrency has ever reached.

8. Market capitalization - the total value of a cryptocurrency calculated by multiplying its current price by its total circulating supply.

9. Pump and dump - a fraudulent practice in which individuals or groups artificially inflate the price of a cryptocurrency through coordinated buying, and then sell off their holdings at a profit.

10. HODL - a term used in the cryptocurrency community to encourage holding onto investments, often in the face of market volatility. It is an acronym for "hold on for dear life."

Supporting Materials

Introduction:

- Nakamoto, S. (2008). Bitcoin: A Peer-to-Peer Electronic Cash System. https://bitcoin.org/bitcoin.pdf

- Buterin, V. (2014). A Next-Generation Smart Contract and Decentralized Application Platform. https://github.com/ethereum/wiki/wiki/White-Paper

Chapter 1:

- Markus, B., & Palmer, J. (2013). Dogecoin. https://github.com/dogecoin/dogecoin/blob/master/READ ME.md

- Buterin, V. (2018). The Meaning of Decentralization. https://medium.com/@VitalikButerin/the-meaning-of-decentralization-a0c92b76a274

Chapter 2:

- Counterparty Foundation. (2017). The Rare Pepe Economy. https://counterparty.io/news/the-rare-pepe-economy/

- CoinDesk. (2017). Rare Pepe Wallet Collects $2,000 in Just 2 Weeks. https://www.coindesk.com/rare-pepe-wallet-collects-2000-just-2-weeks/

Chapter 3:

- BBQCoin Team. (2013). BBQCoin. https://github.com/BBQCoin/BBQCoin/blob/master/READ ME.md

- Antonopoulos, A. M. (2014). Mastering Bitcoin: Unlocking Digital Cryptocurrencies. O'Reilly Media, Inc.

Chapter 4:

- Nyancoin Community. (2014). Nyancoin. https://github.com/Nyancoins/nyancoin/blob/master/README.md

- Popper, N. (2015). Digital Gold: Bitcoin and the Inside Story of the Misfits and Millionaires Trying to Reinvent Money. Harper

Chapter 5:

- HoboNickels Community. (2013). HoboNickels. https://github.com/Tranz5/HoboNickels/blob/master/README.md

- Clark, J. (2014). Altcoin Survey: Building a Better Bitcoin. IEEE Spectrum. https://spectrum.ieee.org/altcoin-survey-building-a-better-bitcoin

Conclusion:

- Yermack, D. (2013). Is Bitcoin a Real Currency? An Economic Appraisal. National Bureau of Economic Research. https://www.nber.org/papers/w19747

- Caplinger, D. (2021). What Are Meme Stocks and How Do You Invest in Them? The Motley Fool. https://www.fool.com/investing/how-to-invest-in-meme-stocks/

www.ingramcontent.com/pod-product-compliance
Lightning Source LLC
Chambersburg PA
CBHW071009050326
40689CB00014B/3553